THOMAS JEFFERSON

Troll Associates

THOMAS JEFFERSON

by Laurence Santrey

Illustrated by Allan Eitzen

Troll Associates

Library of Congress Cataloging in Publication Data

Santrey, Laurence.
    Thomas Jefferson.

    Summary: A biography of the versatile American known
for his accomplishments as inventor, architect, musician,
diplomat, scientific farmer, political philosopher, author
of the Declaration of Independence, and President of the
United States.
    1. Jefferson, Thomas, 1743-1826—Juvenile literature.
2. Presidents—United States—Biography—Juvenile
literature. [1. Jefferson, Thomas, 1743-1826.
2. Presidents] I. Eitzen, Allan, ill. II. Title.
E332.79.S26   1985   973.4'6'0924 [B] [92]   84-2579
ISBN 0-8167-0176-8 (lib. bdg.)
ISBN 0-8167-0177-6 (pbk.)

In all of American history, perhaps no more brilliant and versatile person lived than Thomas Jefferson. Author of the Declaration of Independence, inventor, architect, musician, Vice President and President of the United States, diplomat, scientific farmer, and political philosopher —Jefferson was all of these and more.

7

Thomas Jefferson was born on April 13, 1743, in Albemarle County in the colony of Virginia. His father, Peter, was a wealthy plantation owner. Thomas's mother, Jane, was a member of the aristocratic and wealthy Randolph family of Virginia. The Jefferson estate, called Shadwell, was more than two thousand acres in size. Some of it was farm land, and some of it was forest.

Thomas had six sisters and three brothers. He was the oldest of the boys, which meant that one day he would inherit the entire estate. His early years were spent learning to ride, to hunt, and to fish. As a youngster he also learned to read and write and to play the violin.

Because Mr. Jefferson wanted Tom to be a proper gentleman, he sent the boy to school at the age of nine. Tom's teacher was the Reverend William Douglas. Mr. Douglas instructed young Jefferson in Latin, Greek, and French. Since the school was fifty miles from Shadwell, Tom had to live there for almost nine months of the year. The boy enjoyed learning, but he looked forward to the peaceful summers spent at home.

In 1757, Peter Jefferson died. Tom, who was fourteen years old, now wanted to stay close to his home and family. So he enrolled at a school near Shadwell, run by the Reverend James Maury.

After two years under James Maury's tutelage, Jefferson entered William and Mary College. It was the spring of 1760. There, the tall, redheaded young man blossomed intellectually and socially. Jefferson learned science, mathematics, and ethics under Dr. William Small, a professor of mathematics. Most important of all, he learned logic.

It was Jefferson's ability to think clearly and logically that would make his writing so effective in the years to come. He learned that the most important issues can be stated effectively in the simplest, most direct language.

While he was a student at William and Mary College, Jefferson met George Wythe, a distinguished Virginia lawyer and judge. After graduating from college, Jefferson spent the next five years studying law with Judge Wythe.

Then, in 1767, at the age of twenty-four, Jefferson was admitted to the bar. He began to practice law in Virginia and was an immediate success. But public affairs soon overshadowed Jefferson's law career. In 1769, he was elected a member of the House of Burgesses, which was the name for the Virginia legislature.

As a burgess, Jefferson was not a clever, fiery speaker like his friend, Patrick Henry. However, he won the admiration of his fellow legislators for the clear, logical wording of the laws he wrote. During his service as a Virginia legislator, Jefferson also began to develop the ideas that would grow into the Declaration of Independence.

When Thomas Jefferson first entered the legislature, he saw himself as an Englishman. He was not dissatisfied with the government under which he and his fellow Virginians were living. But the events leading up to the Revolution changed his thoughts and feelings.

The more Great Britain oppressed the Colonies, the more Jefferson questioned the idea of British rule. Eventually, Jefferson joined the group of men crying out for independence, even if it meant war.

In the midst of his political activity,
Jefferson also found time for private
matters. He designed a new home for
himself, called Monticello, and supervised
its constructon. He married Martha Wayles
Skelton, a young widow, and they settled in
their home at Monticello.

Tom and Martha Jefferson had a happy marriage. Mrs. Jefferson gave birth to six children. Unfortunately, she died after ten years of marriage, and only two daughters survived to adulthood. The deaths of those so close to him saddened Thomas Jefferson for the rest of his life.

As the Revolutionary War approached, Jefferson became more deeply involved in colonial politics. In 1775, as a delegate to the Second Continental Congress, he was chosen to be the chief writer for that group.

Jefferson's writing talent was also the reason he was named to a special committee in 1776. This committee was asked to write a declaration of independence. The other members of the committee—John Adams, Benjamin Franklin, Roger Sherman, and Robert Livingston—left the writing to Jefferson. The remarkable document he produced was adopted on July 4, 1776. There were very few changes made by the other members of the Second Continental Congress.

The Declaration, which has become a model for liberty-seeking people everywhere, was stirringly simple. It said, "We hold these truths to be self-evident, that all men are created equal, that they are endowed by their Creator with certain unalienable rights, that among these are life, liberty, and the pursuit of happiness...."

The Declaration of Independence went on to say that governments derive their powers from the people and that when governments are unjust, the people have the right to form new, just governments.

The Declaration set forth all the ways Great Britain had oppressed the Colonies. It ended with the statement that the Colonies were free and independent states and "for the support of this Declaration, with a firm reliance on the protection of divine Providence, we mutually pledge to each other our lives, our fortunes, and our sacred honor."

If Thomas Jefferson had done nothing in his life other than write the Declaration of Independence, he would still be among the greatest Americans in history. But in 1776, his extraordinary career was just beginning. He returned to the Virginia legislature, where he fought for religious freedom and for public education. Jefferson also served two terms as governor of the state, having succeeded Patrick Henry in that office.

In 1783, Thomas Jefferson was elected to the United States Congress. Among his important contributions was the recommendation of a decimal system of money, which is used to this day. He also worked on laws dealing with the territories to the west of the young nation.

Jefferson was Benjamin Franklin's successor as minister to France, and he was President George Washington's first secretary of state. He was also Vice President during the presidency of John Adams. And then, in March 1801, Thomas Jefferson became the third President of the United States.

Jefferson served two terms in the nation's highest office, from 1801 to 1809. Although he lived in the White House, he found it far too large and far too grand for his tastes. This attitude reflected the simple way in which Jefferson tried to live his life.

He wore plain clothing, spoke plainly, and never made a grand display in any way. Jefferson walked to his inauguration rather than ride in a carriage. And he treated all people as equals. Thomas Jefferson was the very embodiment of the democratic ideal.

As President of the United States, Jefferson sent the Lewis and Clark expedition to explore the Louisiana and Northwest Territories. And during his administration, the Louisiana Territory was bought from France, doubling the size of the United States.

After Jefferson completed his second term as President, he happily returned to his home in Monticello. In the years that followed, he enjoyed all the old interests that had delighted him as a younger man. He restored the house and farm fields to their original condition, landscaped the gardens, and began experiments with new farm crops and methods.

Jefferson surrounded himself with his own inventions. These included a swivel chair and a revolving table. There was a seven-day clock, a folding ladder, and a moving pen that made copies of letters as he wrote them.

Jefferson also had time now for two of the greatest interests of his life—books and education. He founded the University of Virginia, and he considered this to be one of his finest accomplishments.

He designed several of its buildings, selected new faculty members, and set up the course of study. Jefferson's own library, which consisted of thousands of books, became the core of the United States Library of Congress.

On July 4, 1826, the fiftieth anniversary of the adoption of the Declaration of Independence, Thomas Jefferson died at Monticello. On his tombstone were inscribed the words he had chosen as his epitaph: "Here was buried Thomas Jefferson, author of the Declaration of American Independence, of the Statute of Virginia for Religious Freedom, and Father of the University of Virginia."